The Best Riddles in the World

George Tam

For the special women in my life, past and present:

To my mother, for giving me life.

To my great-grandmother, for giving her life.

To my wife, for giving me reasons to live a better one.

ACKNOWLEDGMENTS

As a teacher, I am constantly looking for fun ways to challenge my students to learn. I want to engage them in educational activities in which they can play together and use their critical thinking skills to solve problems. It was the inspiration behind this collection of some of the best riddles I have found. Whether you are eight or eighty years old, I hope you will have many hours of pleasure solving these riddles.

What can you catch but never throw?

Clue 1: You pass it from one person to another.
Clue 2: If you get it, you want to get rid of it.
Clue 3: The only way the get rid of it is rest.

Answer: *a cold*

What goes around the world but stays in a corner?

Clue1: It has a square or rectangular shape.
Clue 2: It has numbers written on it.
Clue 3: It has a sticky back.
Clue 4: You send this by putting it in a box.

Answer: *a stamp*

What gets wet the more it dries?

Clue 1: It is soft.
Clue 2: You can fold it.
Clue 3: You may find it in a kitchen or bathroom.

Answer: *a towel*

The more you take, the more you leave behind.

Clue 1: They can be short or long.
Clue 2: The longer they are, the quicker you will be.
Clue 3: They might leave prints.

Answer: *footsteps*

If you drop me, I'm sure to crack. Give me a smile, and I'll always smile back. What am I?

Clue 1: I am a copycat.
Clue 2: People usually see me before they leave home.
Clue 3: I show the reverse.

Answer: *a mirror*

What goes up and down the stairs without moving?

Clue 1: It comes in different colors and patterns.
Clue 2: People walk on it.

Answer: *carpet*

Give me food, and I will live. Give me water, and I will die. What am I?

Clue 1: My color changes.
Clue 2: People build me.
Clue 3: I might be there when you hear a siren.

Answer: *a fire*

What has wheels and flies, but it is not an aircraft?

Clue 1: It visits every home once a week.
Clue 2: People hold their breath when it passes by.
Clue 3: It empties what people no longer want.

Answer: *a garbage truck*

When you have me, you feel like sharing me. But if you do share me, you don't have me. What am I?

Clue 1: You want to hide me.
Clue 2: If you keep me for too long, I want to get out.
Clue 3: If you let me out, I'll lose my power.

Answer: *a secret*

You answer me, although I never ask you questions. What am I?

Clue 1: I might or might not have a "tail".
Clue 2: You pull me close when you speak.
Clue 3: I have holes at both ends.

Answer: *a telephone*

I am light as a feather, yet the strongest man can't hold me for much more than a minute. What am I?

Clue 1: You take me many times a day.
Clue 2: I can be shallow or deep.
Clue 3: I keep you alive.

Answer: *breath*

Use a knife to slice my head and weep beside me when I'm dead. What am I?

Clue 1: I have many layers.
Clue 2: You have to peel off my skin before you use me.
Clue 3: You can make rings out of me.

Answer: *an onion*

What's black when new, red when used, and white when you're through with it?

Clue 1: It comes from the ground.
Clue 2: People use it the most during the summer.
Clue 3: To use it, you have to burn it.

Answer: *charcoal*

I have holes in my top and bottom, my left and right, and in the middle. Yet, I still hold water. What am I?

Clue 1: I look like Swiss cheese, but you can't eat me.
Clue 2: I am always thirsty.
Clue 3: You can find me in the kitchen or bathroom.

Answer: *a sponge*

People need me, but they always give me away. What am I?

Clue 1: I am green.
Clue 2: I have numbers.
Clue 3: You have to give me away in order to get something in return.

Answer: *money*

What belongs to you, but other people use it more than you?

Clue 1: Everyone has one.
Clue 2: You got it when you were born.
Clue 3: You have a first and last one.

Answer: *your name*

A box with no hinges, latch, or lid. Inside a golden treasure is hid. What am I?

Clue 1: I am white on the outside.
Clue 2: I crack under pressure.
Clue 3: People eat me in the morning.

Answer: *an egg*

**No sooner spoken then broken.
What am I?**

Clue 1: You often hear me at night.
Clue 2: What a teacher may ask for.
Clue 3: What you hear the moment before a surprise.

Answer: *silence*

I have three eyes, all in a line. When the red one opens, all freezes until a different one shines. What am I?

Clue 1: I can open my eyes only one at a time.
Clue 2: I look down from high above.
Clue 3: I direct.

Answer: *a traffic light*

Throw it off the highest building, and I'll not break. Put me in the ocean and I will. What am I?

Clue 1: I am light and soft.
Clue 2: People use me the most during the winter.
Clue 3: People take me out during a funeral.

Answer: *a tissue*

I have streets, but no pavement. I have cities, but no buildings. I have forest, but no trees. I have rivers, but no water. What am I?

Clue 1: You might have to unfold me to use.
Clue 2: I am not a legend, but I might have one.
Clue 3: You use me when you're lost.

Answer: *a map*

I can run but not walk. Wherever I go, thought follows me close behind. What am I?

Clue 1: I point.
Clue 2: I might be small or large.
Clue 3: A dog has a wet one.

Answer: *a nose*

You've heard me before, yet you hear me again.
Then I die until you call me again. What am I?

Clue 1: I travel in air.
Clue 2: I come back like a boomerang.
Clue 3: I get bounced around.

Answer: *an echo*

I have no wings, yet I fly. I have no eyes, yet I
cry. Darkness follows me. Lower light I never
see. What am I?

Clue 1: I come down. Then I go back up.
Clue 2: I am made of water.
Clue 3: Sometimes, kids say that I look like cotton candy.

Answer: *a cloud*

There is a green house.

Inside the green house,

there is a white house.

Inside the white,

there is a red house.

Inside the red,

there are many babies.

What am I?

Clue 1: I grow in the ground.
Clue 2: I am juicy.
Clue 3: People eat me during the summer.

Answer: *a watermelon*

Whoever makes it, tells it not. Whoever takes it, knows it not. Whoever knows it, wants it not. What am I?

Clue 1: It is a crime to make me.
Clue 2: It is a crime to knowingly use me.
Clue 3: A store cashier looks closely for me.

Answer: *counterfeit money*

I go in dry and come out wet. The longer I'm in, the stronger I get. What am I?

Clue 1: You can see me through my "clothes".
Clue 2: I usually take a hot "bath" in later afternoon.
Clue 3: You throw me away after I'm done.
Clue 4: You make a drink out of me.

Answer: *a teabag*

A little house full of "meat", no door to go in and eat. What am I?

Clue 1: I am grown on trees.
Clue 2: You have to crack me open.
Clue 3: Crazy people are sometimes named after me.

Answer: *a nut*

**An ancient invention
that is still used today,
Allows people to see through walls,
like Superman in a cape. What am I?**

Clue 1: I am framed.
Clue 2: I am transparent.
Clue 3: I can shatter.

Answer: *a window*

I have an end,

but no beginning,

A home,

but no family,

A space,

without room.

I never speak,

but there is no word I cannot make.

What am I?

Clue 1: I'm attached.
Clue 2: Only one of my keys have a lock.
Clue 3: I have arrows flying up and down, left and right.
Clue 4: I am only as good in spelling as you are.

Answer: *a keyboard*

I go around in circles, but always straight ahead.
Never complain, no matter where I am led.
What am I?

Clue 1: I have no hands or feet.
Clue 2: No one has ever made a square one of me.
Clue 3: I am round.

Answer: *a wheel*

What can run but never walks, has a mouth but
never talks, has a head but never weeps, but has
a bed but never sleeps?

Clue 1: You can jump into it.
Clue 2: Creatures live in it.
Clue 3: You will find the longest one in Egypt.

Answer: *a river*

Who makes it, has no need for it. Who buys it, has no use for it. Who uses it can neither see nor feel it. What is it?

Clue 1: It's a container.
Clue 2: It opens like a clam shell.
Clue 3: You put it in a pit.

Answer: *a coffin*

What runs around the whole yard without moving?

Clue 1: It is made of pieces.
Clue 2: It is driven into the ground.
Clue 3: It divides neighbors.

Answer: *a fence*

I go up

but at the same time go down.

Upwards the blue sky,

and down towards the ground.

I'm present

and past tense too.

So, why don't you come for a ride,

just me and you?

What am I?

Clue 1: I have no seatbelts.
Clue 2: I am not an aircraft.
Clue 3: You find me on the playground.

Answer: *a see-saw*

You throw away the outside and cook the inside. Then you eat the outside and throw away the inside. What is it?

Clue 1: It is sweet.
Clue 2: You eat a snack in a theater made from it.
Clue 3: It is a vegetable.

Answer: *corn*

I am nothing, yet I have value. What am I?

Clue 1: I am not positive or negative.
Clue 2: Below me is extremely cold.
Clue 3: I am oval.
Clue 4: I am a number.

Answer: *zero*

Two bodies have I, though both joined in one.
The stiller I stand, the faster I run. What am I?

Clue 1: My inside is dry.
Clue 2: When I am done, you flip me over.
Clue 3: I measure time.

Answer: *an hourglass*

It's red, blue, purple, and green. No one can reach it, not even the queen. What am I?

Clue 1: I am a band.
Clue 2: I bend.
Clue 3: It is said that you can find a treasure at the end of me.

Answer: *a rainbow*

I am a slippery fish in cloudy sea. Neither hook nor spear will capture me. With your hand you must hunt and seize the fish. To see that it ends up in a dish. What am I?

Clue 1: I'm slippery when wet.
Clue 2: If I touch your eyes, they will burn.
Clue 3: I am a bar.
Clue 4: I keep you clean.

Answer: *soap*

I can be cracked. I can be made. I can be told. I can be played. What am I?

Clue 1: I can make you laugh.
Clue 2: I can make you cry.
Clue 3: Nobody wants to be the center of me.

Answer: *a joke*

I am small as an ant and big as a whale.

I can soar through the air like a bird with a tail.

I can be seen by day and not by night.

I can be seen with a big flash of light.

I follow whoever controls me by the sun, but I
fade away when dark fell like a ton.

What am I?

Clue 1: I'm like your twin, but I don't have a name.
Clue 2: I am tall in the morning, but short at noon.
Clue 3: I follow wherever you go, but I'm not your best
friend.

Answer: *a shadow*

I am used to bat with, yet I never get hit. I am near a ball, yet it is never thrown. What am I?

Clue 1: I am curly.
Clue 2: I protect you.
Clue 3: I have roots.

Answer: *eyelashes*

Thirty-two white horses on a red hill. First, they champ. Then they stamp. Then they stand still. What am I?

Clue 1: I travel up and down.
Clue 2: When I get lost, you will never get me back.
Clue 3: I'm the hardest thing in your body.

Answer: *teeth*

What three letters make a man of a boy?

Clue 1: It goes up but never down.
Clue 2: When you're young, you want it to be higher. When you're old, you want it to be lower.
Clue 3: It is not polite to ask women about theirs.

Answer: *age*

The more there is, the less that you see. Squint all you wish, when surrounded by me. What am I?

Clue 1: I am colorblind.
Clue 2: Burglars are glad to see me.
Clue 3: Children are afraid of me.

Answer: *darkness*

I can be long,

or I can be short.

I can be grown,

or I can be bought.

I can be painted,

or left bare.

I can be round,

or I can be square.

What am I?

Clue 1: You can cut me.
Clue 2: I cure your itch.
Clue 3: Sometimes you bite me.

Answer: *a nail*

**Only two backbones and a thousand ribs.
What am I?**

Clue 1: I am made of wood and steel.
Clue 2: I can be hundreds of miles long.
Clue 3: I twist and turn.
Clue 4: I go over hills and through mountains.

Answer: *railroad track*

**What do you serve but never eat?
What am I?**

Clue 1: Sometimes, I'm trapped in a net like a fish.
Clue 2: I'm green.
Clue 3: I am fuzzy.
Clue 4: I am bouncy.

Answer: *a tennis ball*

Lovely and round,

I shine with pale light.

Grown in the darkness,

A lady's delight.

You see me around,

chained with my brothers.

And if they are lucky,

I'll be worn by mothers.

What am I?

Clue 1: My mother eats waste.
Clue 2: I was made because my mother was irritated.
Clue 3: I live in a shell.

Answer: *a pearl*

What gets whiter the dirtier it gets? What am I?

Clue 1: I am the center of attention.
Clue 2: You find me in the classroom.
Clue 3: I love to teach.
Clue 4: I get dusty.

Answer: *a chalkboard*

What building has the most stories?

Clue 1: You have to be quiet there.
Clue 2: You need a card if you want to check anything out.

Answer: *a library*

All about the house, with his lady he dances. Yet he always works, and never romances. What am I?

Clue 1: I have a long neck but no head.
Clue 2: I keep your house tidy.

Answer: *a broom*

When rain comes down, this goes up. What is it?

Clue 1: It has a metal spine.
Clue 2: People take it out in the sun too.
Clue 3: It keeps you dry.

Answer: *an umbrella*

I weaken all men

for hours each day.

I show you strange visions

while you are away.

I take you by night,

by day take you back.

None suffer to have me,

but do from my lack.

What am I?

Clue 1: The less you have, the more you want.
Clue 2: You can never outlast me.
Clue 3: New parents can never have enough of me.

Answer: *sleep*

I am a "city" that has no people. What am I?

Clue 1: I flow like water.
Clue 2: You can make me by earth, wind, or fire.
Clue 3: I can be shocking, not just on Halloween.

Answer: *electricity*

What ends with 'e' and begins with 'p' and has a thousand letters (two words)?

Clue 1: It's a busy place.
Clue 2: 1st word: Another word for "after".
Clue 3: 2nd word: If you get into trouble, you might be sent to the principal's.

Answer: *a post office*

**What is that over your head but under your hat.
What am I?**

Clue 1: I am dead.
Clue 2: I have a bad day named after me.
Clue 3: People change my color like a chameleon.

Answer: *hair*

**Tear one off and scratch my head. What once
was red is black instead. What am I?**

Clue 1: My body is made of paper or wood.
Clue 2: You strike me.
Clue 3: I light up your life.

Answer: *a match*

What does a man love more than life?

Fear more than death or mortal strife?

What do the poor have, what the rich require?

And what contented men desire? What does

the miser spend,

the spendthrift save?

And all men carry to their grave?

* *mortal strife-* a difficult struggle.

* *miser-* a person who doesn't like to spend money.

* *spendthrift-* a person who loves to buy things.

Clue 1: Having this is better than owing.
Clue 2: You wish this would happen in an accident.
Clue 3: A burglar would be disappointed if he found this.

Answer: *nothing*

What do you throw out to use and take in when you're done?

Clue 1: I touch the floor.
Clue 2: I am heavy.
Clue 3: You use me when you don't want to go anywhere.
Clue 4: I am found on a ship.

Answer: *an anchor*

Poke your fingers in my eyes, and I will open wide my jaws. Linen cloth, quills, or paper, my greedy lust devours them all. What am I?

Clue 1: I come in pairs.
Clue 2: I can't undo what you did.
Clue 3: You have to handle me with care.
Clue 4: I am a tailor's friend.

Answer: *scissors*

What is put on a table and cut, but never eaten? What am I?

Clue 1: I have hearts that don't beat.
Clue 2: I shuffle like an old man, but I have no feet.
Clue 3: A house made of me will fall.

Answer: *a deck of cards*

What has eyes but never sees? What has a tongue but never talks? What has a soul that can't be saved?

Clue 1: My eyelids have no lashes.
Clue 2: My tongue cannot taste, but it breathes.
Clue 3: I always get my tongue tied.
Clue 4: I walk among men.

Answer: a *shoe*

I'm sometimes white,

and always wrong.

I can break a heart

and hurt the strong.

I can build love

and tear it down.

I can make a smile,

but more often bring a frown.

What am I?

Clue 1: I am born out of fear.
Clue 2: I multiply like a virus.
Clue 3: I can never be exposed or I'll die.

Answer: *a lie*

What is it the more you take away, the larger it becomes?

Clue 1: It is an entrance.
Clue 2: It is also an exit.
Clue 3: People fill it.

Answer: *a hole*

Whom do people gaze at with an open mouth? Who am I?

Clue 1: I might put you to sleep.
Clue 2: I might push and pull.
Clue 3: I wear a white coat.

Answer: *a dentist*

Metal, bone, or plastic I may be. Many teeth I have and always bared. Yet my bite harms no one and ladies delight in my touch. What am I?

Clue 1: You might want to use me after a rollercoaster ride.
Clue 2: If you need a wig, you probably don't have me.

Answer: *a comb*

I love to dance and twist and prance. I shake my tail, away I sail. Wingless, I fly into the sky. What am I?

Clue 1: My skeleton is on the outside.
Clue 2: I am attached to you.
Clue 3: I rise to the occasion.

Answer: *a kite*

Pronounced as one letter,

but written with three.

Two letters there are,

and only two in me.

I'm double, I'm single.

I'm black, blue, and gray.

I'm read from both ends,

and the same either way.

What am I?

Clue 1: I am round.
Clue 2: I may become cloudy in my old age.
Clue 3: I am a ball, but I don't bounce.

Answer: *eye*

I am a warrior amongst the flowers, bearing a thrusting sword. Able and ready to use it to guard my golden horde. What am I?

Clue 1: After I use my sword, I will die.
Clue 2: I store my food in a comb.

Answer: *a bee*

What has 4 legs in the morning, 2 legs in the afternoon, and 3 legs in the evening?

Clue 1: baby
Clue 2: child
Clue 3: adult

Answer: *a man*

A father's child, a mother's child, yet no one's son. Who am I?

Clue 1: female
Clue 2: sister
Clue 3: daddy's girl

Answer: *a daughter*

I'm where yesterday follows today, and tomorrow's in the middle. What am I?

Clue 1: pages
Clue 2: (alphabetical) order
Clue 3: a book

Answer: *a dictionary*

Weight in my belly. Trees on my back. Nails in my ribs. Feet I do lack. What am I?

Clue 1: I rock and roll.
Clue 2: I can only go forward.
Clue 3: I float.

Answer: *a boat*

What's the only room from which no one can enter or leave. What am I?

Clue 1: I have a cap.
Clue 2: I grow in the ground.
Clue 3: People mistakenly call me a vegetable.

Answer: *a mushroom*

When I take off my clothes, it puts on its clothes.
When I put on my clothes, it takes off its clothes.
What is it?

Clue 1: It has a hook.
Clue 2: It is found in a closet.

Answer: *a hanger*

I am a key that cannot open a lock. I live in
harmony with many others like me. I make a
solitary sound when you tickle me. What am I?

Clue 1: I'm white.
Clue 2: I'm black.
Clue 3: I'm wired.

Answer: *a piano key*

You get many of me,

but never enough.

After the last one,

your life soon will snuff.

You may have one of me,

but one day a year.

When the last one is gone,

your life disappears.

What am I?

Clue 1: The young and the old all have me.
Clue 2: I always arrive on time every year.

Answer: *a birthday*

When set loose, I fly away. Never so cursed as I go astray. What am I?

Clue 1: I might announce my arrival quietly or loudly.
Clue 2: I am not a welcomed guest. When I arrive, people leave.

Answer: *a fart*

The beginning of eternity, the end of time and space. The beginning of every end, and the end of every place. What am I?

Clue 1: I am in an alphabet soup.
Clue 2: I am a vowel.

Answer: *the letter 'e'*

My voice is tender, my waist is slender, and I'm often invited to play. Yet wherever I go, I must take my bow or else I have nothing to say. What am I?

Clue 1: Sometimes, I tune out.
Clue 2: Cello and bass are in my family.

Answer: *a violin*

What is coming, but never arrives?

Clue 1: It's what a lazy person often says.
Clue 2: After it has arrived, you can look back on today.

Answer: *tomorrow*

A little pool

with two layers

of wall around it,

One white and soft

and the other

dark and hard,

Amidst a light brown

grassy lawn

with an outline

of a green grass. What am I?

Clue 1: I could be a flake.
Clue 2: You can make a kind of milk out of me.
Clue 3: You pick me from a tree.

Answer: *a coconut*

They have not flesh, nor feathers, nor scales, nor bone. Yet they have fingers and thumbs of their own. What are they?

Clue 1: A burglar's tool.
Clue 2: You wear these.

Answer: *gloves*

They come witness the night without being called, a sailor's guide and a poet's tears. They are lost to sight each day without the hand of a thief. What are we?

Clue 1: We are countless.
Clue 2: We are burning hot.
Clue 3: Celebrities are sometimes called these.

Answer: *stars*

It doesn't bark, it doesn't bite, but it still doesn't let you in the house. What is it?

Clue 1: It turns.
Clue 2: It has a hole.

Answer: *a lock*

I have married many, but have never been married. Who am I?

Clue 1: I'm a man.
Clue 2: I stand above the crowd.
Clue 3: I say vows that people make.

Answer: *a priest*

I have no voice,

yet I speak to you.

I tell of all things in the world that people do.

I have leaves,

but I'm not a tree.

I have a spine and hinges,

but I am not a man or a door.

I have told you all,

and I can't tell you more.

What am I?

Clue 1: You hold me in your hands.
Clue 2: I am made from a tree.
Clue3: You can read my mind.

Answer: *a book*

My life can be measured in hours. I serve by being devoured. Thin, I am quick. Fat, I am slow. Wind is my foe. What am I?

Clue 1: You take me out in an emergency.
Clue 2: I melt like ice cream.
Clue 3: I allow you to see in darkness.

Answer: *a candle*

What comes once in a minute, twice in a moment, but never in a thousand year?

Clue 1: A well-known candy has it in its name.
Clue 2: This letter makes a sound that you might hear during a good meal.

Answer: *letter 'm'*

When you are sad, you tear out my inside. When I'm finished, you crush my outsides.
What am I?

Clue 1: My belly is stuffed.
Clue 2: My belly is wide open.
Clue 3: My guts stick out of my belly.

Answer: *a tissue box*

Lighter than what I am made of, more of me is hidden than is seen, I am the bane of the mariner, a tooth within the sea. What am I?

* bane-something that causes distress or worry
* mariner- a sailor

Clue 1: I am made of water.
Clue 2: I can be as tall as a mountain.

Answer: *an iceberg*

I can sizzle like bacon,

I am made with an egg.

I have plenty of backbone,

but lack a good leg.

I peel layers like onions,

but still remain whole.

I can be long

like a flagpole,

yet fit in a hole.

What am I?

Clue 1: I am deaf.
Clue 2: I don't chew, but can only swallow.
Clue 3: I smell with my tongue.

Answer: *a snake*

I travel by foot, but I am toeless. No matter where I go, I'm never far from home. What am I?

Clue 1: Wherever I go, I leave a trail.
Clue 2: Some people like to eat me.
Clue 3: I hide in my shell.

Answer: *a snail*

I build up castles. I tear down mountains. I make some men blind. I help others to see. What am I?

Clue 1: I am tiny, but I can make grown men cry.
Clue 2: Furniture makers use a paper made of me.
Clue 3: You can find me on a beach.

Answer: *sand*

What fastens two people yet touches only one?
What am I?

* fasten- to hold together

Clue 1: I am round, but I have no top or bottom.
Clue 2: Couples exchange my twin and me.

Answer: *a wedding ring*

The higher I climb, the hotter I engage. I
cannot escape my crystal cage. What am I?

Clue 1: I am an instrument, but not a musical one.
Clue 2: I am used for measuring.
Clue3: I go up and down from day to night.

Answer: *a thermometer*

I am so small,

and sometimes I'm missed.

I get misplaced, misused,

and help you when you list.

People usually pause

when they see me,

So you can tell me

what I could be?

Clue 1: I have a tail.
Clue 2: I tell you to slow down, but I'm not a traffic cop.
Clue 3: I have a life sentence.
Clue 4: I am a mark.

Answer: *a comma*

I have many feathers to help me fly. I have a body and head, but I'm not alive. It is your strength which determines how far I go. You can hold me in your hand, but I'm never thrown. What am I?

Clue 1: When I'm crooked, I am useless.
Clue 2: I go to Target, not the store.

Answer: *an arrow*

Liquid cannot pass me through, yet liquid I spew if you make me move. Cover I do something very complex, yet I am very easy to flex. What am I?

Clue 1: I come in different shades of color.
Clue 2: I am an organ, but I don't make a sound.
Clue 3: If you are not easily rattled, people say you have thick one.

Answer: *skin*

What can bring back the dead, make us laugh, make us young, born in an instant, yet lasts a life time? What are they?

Clue 1: They are like home movies.
Clue 2: The more recent the events, the clearer they are.

Answer: *memories*

It may only be given, not taken or bought, what the sinner desires, but the saint does not. What am I?

Clue 1: I am a gift.
Clue 2: I am something you can ask for, but can never be demanded.

Answer: *forgiveness*

I am a word

of meanings three.

Three ways of spelling me there be.

The first is an odor,

a smell if you will.

The second some money,

but not in a bill.

The third is a past tense,

a method of passing things on or around.

Can you tell me now,

what these words are

that have the same sound?
(3 answers)

Clue 1: 1st word- fragrance
Clue 2: 2nd word- a coin
Clue 3: 3rd word- already left

Answer: *scent, cent, sent*

What falls but never breaks and breaks but never falls? What are we (2 answers)**?**

Clip 1: We are two strangers.
Clip 2: We are opposites.
Clip 3: We are bright and dark.

Answer: *day and night*

I am so simple, that I can only point. Yet I guide men all over the world. What am I?

Clue 1: I am round.
Clue 2: I always point north.
Clue 3: I am a sailor's tool.

Answer: *a compass*

Often held but never touched, always wet but never rust, often bites but seldom bit, to use me well you must use wit. **What am I?**

Clue 1: Like fingerprints, everyone's unique.
Clue 2: I am the strongest muscle in the body.
Clue 3: I have many bumps.

Answer: *a tongue*

Toss me out of the window, you'll find a grieving wife, pull me back through the door, and watch someone give life! **What are we (2 answers)?**

Clue 1: 1st word- a surviving spouse
Clue 2: 2nd word- a generous person

Answer: *widow, donor*

I am a word 5 letters,

and people eat me.

If you remove the first letter,

I become a form of energy.

Remove the first two,

and I'm needed to live.

Scramble the last 3,

and you can drink me.

What am I?

Clue 1: 1st word- a kind of bread
Clue 2: 2nd word- needed for cooking
Clue 3: 3rd word- you can gorge or nibble
Clue 4: 4th word- it can be drank hot or cold

Answer: *wheat, heat, eat, tea*

I am two-face, but bear only one. I have no legs, but travel widely. Men spill much blood over me. Kings leave their imprint on me. I have greatest power when given away, yet lust for me keeps me locked away. What am I?

Clue 1: We clank if there are two or more of me together.
Clue 2: You can toss me and make a call.

Answer: *a coin*

What is round as a hoop, deep as a pail, never sings out until it's grabbed by the tail?

Clue 1: It's found at some missions or churches.
Clue 2: Fill in the blanks in which the word is used: ___hop; ____ bottoms
Clue 3: It rings.

Answer: *a bell*

The first is a person who lives in disguise,

who deals in secret and tells nothing but lies.

Then think of a letter that's last to mend

the middle of middle and end of end.

Now think of a sound which is often heard

in search of every unknown word.

Put it together and answer me this…

Which creature would you be unwilling to

kiss?

Clue 1: Combine all the parts to reveal the answer.
Clue 2: 1st part- a secret agent
Clue 3: 2nd part- a passing grade
Clue 4: 3rd part- a suffix that means " a person who…"

Answer: *spider*

I am often sought after

but seldom found.

Some people never find me

until they are in the ground.

Arguing nations find me

hard to find.

Yet often, I am just a state of mind.

Some believe I can only be found

by divine intervention from above.

Another name for me is Love.

What am I?

Clue 1: I am stillness.
Clue 2: I am harmony.

Answer: *peace*

Some try to hide,

some try to cheat,

but time will show,

we always will meet.

Try as you might,

to guess my name.

I promise you'll know,

when you I do claim.

What am I?

Clue 1: I come at the end.
Clue 2: No one can avoid me.
Clue 3: I am the final destination.

Answer: *death*

Without a body, nor a beak. Clipped, but flaps in the wind and dresses for a week. What am I?

Clue 1: You find me in the backyard.
Clue 2: I hang out only when it's a sunny day.
Clue 3: I have lines like telephone poles.

Answer: *clothesline*

We are the names of three consecutive days, but we are none of the days of the week. What are we (3 answers)?

Clue 1: 1st word- Past
Clue 2: 2nd word- Present
Clue 3: 3rd word- Future

Answer: *Yesterday, today, tomorrow*

What is wider

than life itself,

longer than forever,

So simple

it's complicated,

Travels but never

leaves a spot,

Puts others in danger,

but no one gets hurt,

And reaches to worlds unknown.

What am I?

Clue 1: I'm limitless.
Clue 2: I'm creative.
Clue 3: I am born in your mind.

Answer: *your imagination*

I am very easily missed,

And often overlooked.

I come to some people,

Others must search.

Once you find me,

you must take advantage.

For I may be gone,

before you know.

What am I?

Clue 1: chance
Clue 2: luck
Clue 3: preparation

Answer: *opportunity*

You must keep this thing,
its loss will affect your brothers.
For once yours is lost,
it will soon be lost by others.
What is it?

Clue 1: a mood
Clue 2: heats up and cools down
Clue 3: poise

Answer: *your temper*

Nearly dark as the sun,
sometimes dark as space,
Like a pearl on black velvet
with diamonds,
twinkling in a case.
What am I?

Clue 1: You can only see one side of me.
Clue 2: I am a satellite or orbit.
Clue 2: I can be new, full, or blue

Answer: *a moon*

The sun bakes them, the hand breaks them, the foot treads on them, and the mouth tastes them. What are we?

Clue 1: We are green or red.
Clue 2: We have a skin.
Clue 3: You make us into a drink.

Answer: *grapes*

Although my cow is dead, I still beat her. What a racket she makes! What is it?

Clue 1: It's white.
Clue 2: It vibrates.
Clue 3: You beat it with sticks, but it won't get hurt.

Answer: *a drum*

ABOUT THE AUTHOR

George Tam is an educator and a photographer living near
Los Angeles, California.

Made in the USA
Middletown, DE
06 August 2017